-Graces-
for all Occasions

GW00601965

by
Ivan Street

MOORLEY'S B
I
& Bookshop Ltd.
L
E

Book illustrations by: Jane Elizabeth Martin

MOORLEY'S B I & Bookshop Ltd.
L E

23 Park Road, Ilkeston
Derbys. DE7 5DA
Tel: (0602) 320643

ISBN 0 86071 240 0

GRACES FOR ALL OCCASIONS

"Necessity is the mother of invention"

My graces were written purely by circumstances. Over many years and on lots of occasions I have been asked to commence proceedings. To avoid repetition I started to write my own material, and people enjoyed being part of it. They told me so and asked for copies. I have therefore decided to put my thoughts and prayers on to paper. Hope you enjoy pronouncing Grace and I trust your friends will listen too.

Every Blessing.

I.E.S.

P.S. Just a help! Select the grace you wish to use for the occasion, copy it out on to a small card. Hold the card in the palm of your hand. It gives confidence - I know!

For Gloria with my love.

NO. 1.

Right and correct it is to sing,
Grateful praise to our Heavenly King.
All things living God will feed.
His full bounty supplies their need.
At this time and in this place,
Accept these thanks in our small grace.

                                        Amen.

NO. 2.

Lord we thank You, for the pleasure of dining.
For excellent food, and first class wining.
As our time continues with music and dancing,
May our life be full of praise enhancing.

                                        Amen.

NO. 3.

Eating out is a real pleasure.
Sheer joy of being together.
No food to cook.
No meal to serve.
Thank You Lord for this delight,
Accept our prayer for a lovely night.

                                        Amen.

NO. 4.

 Lord, for friendship, fellowship,
  fun and food, we thank You.
Bless our meal now we pray.

      Amen.

NO. 5.

    For starter, main course, sweet,

                and the toast.

    Praise Father, Son and Holy Ghost.

                        Amen.

NO. 6.

    Lord, lunch is halfway through our day.

    For good fresh salads we have to say;

    Thank You so for variety that surrounds

    In all Thy love that so abounds.

                        Amen.

NO. 7.

    We thank You Lord for our daily meat,

    These tables full with goods to eat.

    Glasses brimming with wine to drink,

    Praise to God, and may we think

    Of all the folk whose talents we employ.

    God Bless them all, and give them joy.

                        Amen.

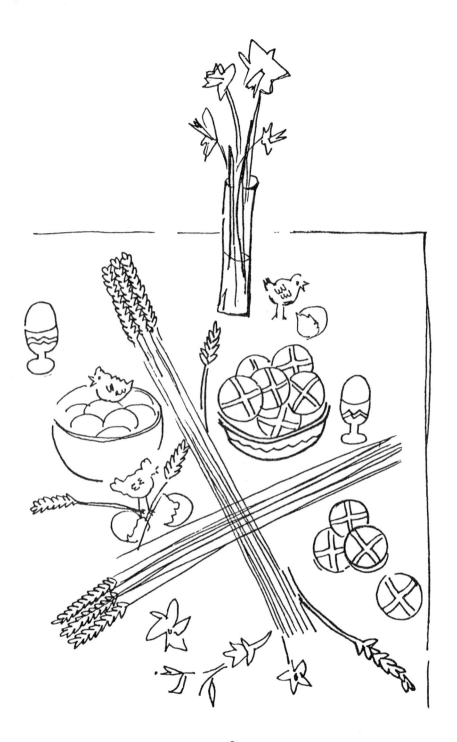

NO. 8.

Bread and water is our basic need,
Looking around Lord, what a feed.
Much above our want and care,
Take our thanks in this prayer.
Bless our time together.

Amen.

NO. 9.

Meeting together on this Special Day,
Bless our company now we pray.
Let us partake of food so fine
And offer our thanks to God Divine.

Amen.

NO. 10.

Our dishes full of salad fare.
How good Lord to see Your ware.
Of nature used for man's delight,
Our grateful thanks for a lovely sight.
May we enjoy now the feast You give,
And praise Your greatness as we live.

Amen.

NO. 11.

> Assembled amongst this appetising array,
> Let us offer our thanks while we may.
> Remembering with gratitude as we say,
> Praise be to God on this Special Day.

> Amen.

NO. 12.

> O Lord may we wish,
> Whatever is put upon our dish.
> Our satisfaction can be met,
> And contentment will then let
> Our thanks to You be said,
> For having once again us fed.

> Amen.

NO. 13.

> Father, we thank You for our daily bread.
> May we not be crusty or stale, but tasty
> and fresh in all that we do. Be amongst
> our fellowship now we ask.

> Amen.

NO. 14.

 All on the table waiting there,
 To be eaten after this prayer.
 It looks so good we'll not delay,
 So accept our Grace Lord for this day.

Amen.

NO. 15.

Accept our Grace, so full of praise

For all the food the table displays.

We sing a happy song foretelling

Of well spoken words, and laughter swelling.

The music then gay, a marvellous ball.

What a happy time was had by all.

Amen.

NO. 16.

On the Lord's name we call,

You are the maker of it all.

When we look around, we see

The greatness and the mystery,

Of all the food we now receive,

Make us in our hearts believe,

That You give love to each one now,

As in this grace we humbly bow.

Amen.

NO. 17.

Eat to live, or live to eat.

We thank You for our daily meat.

In this our grace,

Short though it be,

Accept our praise for all we see.

Amen.

NO. 18.

     For simple things like bread and butter,

     May we never fail to utter

     Our sincere thanks now quietly said,

     To the Lord of Peace our natural Head.

                         Amen.

NO. 19.

>For bread and butter, jam and cakes,
>Let us thank our God who makes,
>All things lovely for us to feed,
>And every day supplies our need.
>Each afternoon like this well spent,
>With friendships moulded heaven sent.
>Bless our fellowship together.
>
>Amen.

NO. 20.

>Lord accept our praise in verbal ballad.
>For the crisp and newness of fresh salad.
>Give us those qualities describing our dish,
>And make us alive, and tuned to your wish.
>
>Amen.

NO. 21.

>Thanks for food to give us health,
>Supplied around from Nature's wealth.
>At this table to meet our need,
>Accept our praise for this feed.
>We feel good as Your blessings flow,
>May we ever in Your love grow.
>
>Amen.

NO. 22.

Whilst we stand around this table
With happy hearts, now make us able
To offer our wishes around the room,
Asking Your blessing on bride and groom.
Make this a time for remembrance too,
As we offer this our praise to You.

Amen.

NO. 23.

God speaks to us and shows His Hand,
With our tables full from the land.
As we thank Him quietly now,
And in anticipation numbly bow,
Let us enjoy our meal so new,
Remaining in friendship ever true.

Amen.

NO. 24.

> For all the good things of the soil,
> Available to us as men toil.
> Our table full of goods we see,
> Make us grateful unto Thee.
> Accept Father, our thoughts and
> prayers at this time.
>
> Amen.

NO. 25.

> Cornflakes, toast, and marmalade,
> Given by one who all things made.
> Egg and bacon, beans and bread,
> So supplied that we can be fed.
> Thanks for breakfast - a real delight.
> Praise to our Lord God of the light.
>
> Amen.

NO. 26.

> Lord, remembering the miracle at Cana.
> May we not be like water; colourless,
> odourless and tasteless, but like wine;
> sparkling, aromatic, full of life.
> Bless our feasting together tonight.
>
> Amen.

NO. 27.

What we see is heaven sent,
A table full of nourishment.
Go eat, enjoy, and have your fill,
For that's God's wish and His will.
Thank You Father and Bless our meal
together now.
Amen.

NO. 28.

Praise God from whom all blessings flow,
Thank Him who maketh all things grow,
Accept our prayers for daily bread,
And making sure that we're well fed.
Amen.

NO. 29.

We stand together with one voice,
And bow our heads to rejoice,
Giving thanks for food seen here,
With lovely choices made so clear.
This our praise in trust secure,
For Thy promise ever sure;
To give us always daily bread,
Accept these prayers together said.
Amen.

NO. 30.

>For our table tonight,
>And all that will fill it.
>Praise Father, Son, and Holy Spirit.
>>Amen.

NO. 31.

>Father, for the produce of the Earth,
>That You have given us from our birth,
>On this occasion we all rejoice
>For food and drink, and in one voice
>We give You thanks on high above,
>And eat together in Your love.
>>Amen.

NO. 32.

>For eats which now upon us shower,
>Father we thank You for Your power,
>To fill our table, and make us praise
>As You show us Your kindly ways.
>Bless our meal together.
>>Amen.

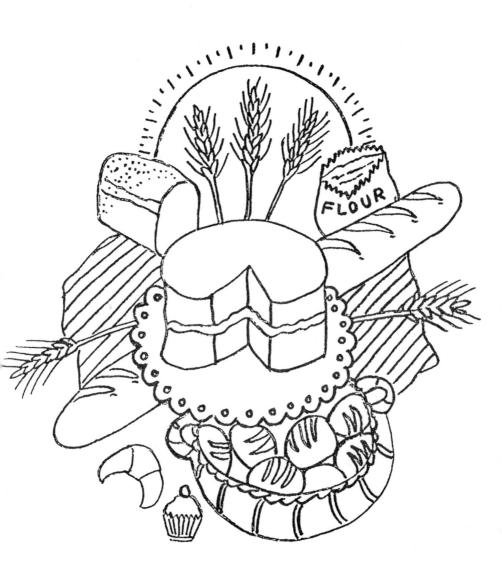

NO. 33.

   Lord God, You still hear our cry,
   Thank You for this food supply.
   This table full of rich delight,
   To eyes that love a feastly sight,
   Accept our praise for every bite
   For taste, with smell and appetite.

                              Amen.

                    ———

NO. 34.

   Father may we never fail,
   As Thy goodness doth prevail,
   To thank You for our daily bread,
   Therefore accept our grace now said.
   Take the thoughts in our mind,
   That appreciate Your gifts so kind.

                              Amen.

                    ———

NO. 35.

   Looking on our tables there,
   The food abounds to take our share,
   With friends around us everywhere,
   We praise and thank You for Your care.
   Leading us where we cannot see,
   Accept our grace Lord full and free.

                              Amen.

NO. 36.

> May the earth be better because we are here,
> Let us all work together with good cheer.
> Now feast and drink while in this place,
> And be aware of God's good grace.

Amen.

NO. 37.

> We meet as one on this special day,
> And all together with Grace say,
> Thank You Father for our feed,
> For giving us meals to meet our need.
> The table full to our demands,
> The work of many peoples' hands.
> Accept our prayers.

Amen.

NO. 38.

> As we bow our heads Lord let's reflect
> On people who give in their entire
> For provision of food and all we require.
> Accept our praise for a lovely meal.
> The coffee and wine and all the drink,
> Take this our grace and make us think.

Amen.

NO. 39.

With Grace we do lead,

Let us stand and take heed.

As Your love's understood,

For all things so good,

Our thanks we now bring,

And Your praises we sing.

                    Amen.

NO. 40.

Whatever happens, and always so,

Our food is ever there we know.

We thank You for the times all spread,

From morn until we go to bed.

For all the meals of every day;

Dinner, tea, come what may.

Accept our Grace, dear Lord.

                    Amen.

NO. 41.

Accept this grace now offered,

For all the food imparts,

Take what You most desirest,

Our grateful, thankful hearts.

All this refreshment given us

Is sent from God above.

Thank You Lord, Thank You Lord,

For all Your love.

                    Amen.

NO. 42.

Praise we the chefs and cooks of skill,
Rich in art, made richer still,
By bringing together friendly hands,
People of many climes and clans.
As we eat assembled their super dishes,
Accept our Grace Father with loving wishes.

Amen.

NO. 43.

For all our meals Lord, food and drink,
Accept our thanks and make us think,
Of all the work in kind and deed,
So necessary to provide our need.
Be at our table now as we pray
And by our side always, every day.

Amen.

NO. 44.

Accept this grace as Your due,
Now in our best we stand to You.
Thanks for the blessings of this night
For food and drink within our sight.

Amen.

NO. 45.

Lamb and beef and the royal roast,
May we never forget to toast
Our absent friends, not with us now,
Remembering them always as we bow.
Collect the memories in our grace,
Accept our thanks while in this place.

Amen.

NO. 46.

Hot drinks and biscuits for our supper.
Let us ever keep it upper
In our minds to give You thought,
For all the fun that You have brought,
Accept our prayer and warm our heart
Make us ever ready a fresh day to start.

Amen.

NO. 47.

We find ourselves now on the beach.
The sand and sea Lord how they preach.
We're looking forward to picnic lunch,
Bless us together - what a bunch.
But thanks we give for all to see
Accept our grace and make us free.

Amen.

NO. 48.

Now arisen from our slumber,
Having had a night in bed,
Take this grace amongst our number,
Acknowledging You to be the head.
Thank You for breakfast on this day
Accept our gratefulness we say.

Amen.

NO. 49.

Now let our voice be one of praise,
For happy hours and super days.
In this moment eating now,
As together we gently bow,
Bless our food we richly see
And touch our hearts Lord - even me.

Amen.

NO. 50.

It is good to do the Father's will,
To bow in grace so quiet and still.
And thank Him for a lovely tea,
The friends and all around we see.
Take our prayers, it's our delight,
Bless all the people in Your sight.

Amen.

NO. 51.

Bless our meal we now implore,
Stay by our side for evermore.
We thank You Lord whatever state,
For all the things You cultivate.
All fruit and veg. that You provide
And being along our way the guide.

Amen.

NO. 52.

Lord we need Your tender care.
Thank You for food that You prepare.
Give us each day our daily bread,
To keep us fit and well fed.
Now together as we meet,
Accept our praise to take a seat.

Amen.

NO. 53.

O Lord, may we not be in haste,
To over eat; and out of taste.
Looking lovely, dressed to kill,
Waiting eagerly to have our fill.
Let's take sufficient - only just
Avoiding clothes that groan and bust,
We say our grace to thank You now
Remembering this our commonsense vow
To only eat enough to seek
A return booking for all next week.

Amen.

NO. 54.

In grace we give You thanks and praise,
For happy times and enjoyable days.
Vegetables and fruit Your love declare,
When meals are eaten You are there.

Amen.

NO. 55.

Speak dear Lord to every ear,
As Thy full bounty doth appear.
Looking around is a real pleasure,
A table full of top chef's treasure.
All the produce of the land,
Eaten now as from Your Hand.
Bless our meal together.

Amen.

NO. 56.

Lord above it's heaven sent,
The coming of this great event.
Meeting friends from far and wide,
Sitting together on every side.
Accept our prayers said in this grace
For all the food now in its place.

Amen.

NO. 57.

Soup or melon to begin,
Meat with dressing, then we win.
Sweets from the table now with ease,
Finish off with choice of cheese.
For all this food now in its place
Accept our thankful words of grace.

Amen.

NO. 58.

Take our thanks as we now dine,
For all Your gifts including wine.
Around our table with friends who care
Let us all together share,
In serving others which demands
A few kind words and helping hands.
So take our thoughts in this prayer
And may we all together fare.

Amen.

NO. 59.

Make us in your presence still,
As we acknowledge grain from the mill.
It gives us flour, bread, and cake,
That in Your wisdom all things make.
At this table full of kind
We praise You with a gladsome mind.

Amen.

NO. 60.

    Accept our praise in grace said now,
As we before You grateful bow.
With lips and lives we gladly show,
For in Your fellowship we go
Enjoying fun and food with friends,
And all the gifts the good God sends.

                        Amen.
